First published in 2014
by Singing Dragon
an imprint of Jessica Kingsley Publishers
73 Collier Street
London N1 9BE, UK
and
400 Market Street, Suite 400
Philadelphia, PA 19106, USA

www.singingdragon.com

Copyright © Sigrún Daníelsdóttir 2014
Illustrations copyright © Björk Bjarkadóttir 2014

Library of Congress Cataloging in Publication Data
A CIP catalog record for this book is available from the Library of Congress

British Library Cataloguing in Publication Data
A CIP catalogue record for this book is available from the British Library

ISBN 978 1 84819 228 7
eISBN 978 0 85701 178 7

Printed and bound in China

Sigrún Daníelsdóttir

Your Body is Awesome

Body respect for children

Illustrations by

Björk Bjarkadóttir

SINGING
DRAGON

For my children,
Silja, Rökkvi and Pétur

Everybody has a body.

We live in our body.

It is like our house.

Bodies are amazing instruments that allow us to do all sorts of exciting things.

Bodies are fun.

Like jumping up and down, dancing, and splashing.

Our body can make us feel good.

Like when we get a foot massage.

Or snuggle up on the sofa.

Or when someone strokes our back at bedtime.

It's nice to have a body.

Bodies are smart.

They let us know what they need to stay well and feel good.

Bodies don't use words to talk to us. They use feelings.
They send us messages about what they need through the
way we feel.

When we feel hungry, our body is telling us that it needs food.

GR...

When we feel full, our body is telling us it has had enough for now.

When we feel tired, our body is telling us that it needs rest.

When we wake up feeling refreshed.

our body is telling us it is fully rested.

It is important to listen to our bodies. What happens, for instance, if our body lets us know that it needs to go to the bathroom and we don't listen?

It is also important that adults listen to us when we tell them what is happening in our body. When we say that we are full, or tired, or need to use the bathroom, adults should listen. Our body knows best.

Try closing your eyes and traveling down into your tummy.

How do you feel in there? Is your stomach hungry?

Full? Or neither?

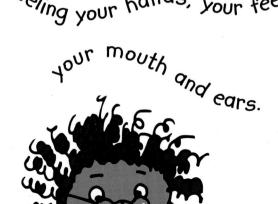

Try feeling your hands, your feet,

Stretch out your toes and fingers in every direction.

your mouth and ears.

When you breathe deeply, feel the way the air comes in through your nose and goes down into your lungs and then goes back out the same way.

This is your body. It is amazing.

Your body is brilliant.

It makes your heart beat and the blood pump through your veins.

It digests your food and grows bigger and stronger every day.

It makes your hair and nails grow, it heals your cuts and bruises, and fights illness and infections.

Your body is a good body.

Bodies need a lot of care.

They need nutritious food to grow bigger and have the energy to do everything they need to do all day.

They need lots of fun and activity in order to stay healthy and have strong muscles and bones.

They need to get plenty of rest at night so that they will be refreshed and ready for action the next day.

And they need time, and sometimes help, to heal when they get sick or hurt.

Every body is different.

Some bodies are taller and others are shorter.

Some bodies are larger and others are smaller.

Some have curly hair and others straight.

Some have dark skin and others fair.

Every body is unique.

Just imagine if human beings were flowers.
Wouldn't it be boring if all the flowers in the
world were the same? We want to have all sorts
of flowers so that we can make a beautiful,
colorful, big bunch of flowers.

We also want there to be all sorts of birds
and animals.

And we think it's much more fun to color with lots
of crayons instead of just one.

It's wonderful that everything is so different.

All bodies are good bodies.

A tall body is not better than a short body—
they are just different.

Fat and thin bodies are also different.
Neither is better than the other.
They are just different.

Like pink and green.

Or tulips and daisies.

It is important to feel good about your body and be happy about the way you are.

It is also important to allow others to be happy about the way they are.

We don't need to be like anybody but ourselves.

Be kind to your body and treat it with love.

Your body is your friend and you will live in it all your life.

A MESSAGE FOR ADULTS

This book is written for children and the adults who care for them in the hope of promoting healthy body image and respect for diversity. Children's body image is part of their general self-image and therefore it is important that they grow up in an environment that helps them see their bodies in a positive way. Even though it is obvious that people come in different shapes and sizes, we live in an environment that doesn't always respect this fact. As a result, many people feel uncomfortable in their skin and think they should be different from how they are.

This is a cause for concern because children's body image has a powerful influence on their health and well-being. Children and adolescents who are dissatisfied with their bodies are at an increased risk of having lower self-esteem and various mental health problems. Young people with a negative body image are also more likely to develop unhealthy behaviours—they are often less physically active and have unhealthier eating habits than kids who are happier with their bodies. We take better care of the things we love and so it is important for children to learn to love their bodies from the very start.

For children to be able to develop a positive body image, their bodies need to be accepted in the world around them. That is why body diversity needs to be embraced as a normal part of life and met with the same respect and inclusion we try to promote in other areas of human diversity. We should speak openly to children about all bodies being different and teach them that this diversity is a natural and positive aspect of human existence.

This does not mean we should be indifferent about children's health. Quite the contrary. We want children to learn that their bodies are precious and need care. It is important for them to get to know their bodies, maintain curiosity about them, and learn to listen and respond to the signals their bodies send them. But these are things children need to learn on their own terms, guided by self-care. Children should never be led to believe that there is something wrong with their bodies or the bodies of others.

All children have a right to feel good in their skin and be proud of themselves the way they are.

Björk Bjarkadóttir was born in Iceland but now lives in Oslo. Her current projects include writing children's books, illustration, graphic design and photography.

For more information,
www.bjorkbjarka.no

ABOUT THE AUTHOR

Sigrún Daníelsdóttir is a psychologist specializing in body image and eating issues. She believes all bodies are created equal and that kids should be supported in being happy in their own, unique skin.

For more information,
www.facebook.com/bodyrespectforchildren